DOG HACKS HANDBOOK

HOW TO RAISE YOUR BEST FRIEND TO BE THE HAPPIEST & HEALTHIEST PUP EVER

DRAGON FRUIT

MARIA LLORENS AND HUGO VILLABONA

Front Cover Image: kavalenkava volha/shutterstock.com
Back Cover Image: microvector/shutterstock.com &
macrovector/shutterstock.com
Cover Design Elina Diaz
Interior Design, Theme and Layout: Elina Diaz & Laura Mejia
All icons and illustrations when not defined were provided via
www.shutterstock.com & www.nounproject.com.

Hugo Villabona and Maria Llorens /Mango Media, Inc.
2525 Ponce de Leon, Suite 300
Coral Gables, FL 33134
www.mangomedia.us

Publisher's Note: This is a work of nonfiction. Some names, locations and
identifying details may have been changed at the author and/or publishers
discretion. The authors wish to thank all the experts, guides and experiences
that helped shape the story.

Dog Hacks Handbook: How to Raise Your Best Friend to be the Happiest
and Healthiest Pup Ever / Hugo Villabona and Maria Llorens. -- 1st ed.
ISBN 978-1-63353-127-7

DISCLAIMER

Owning your first dog can be overwhelming, but we've broken down all the basics from housebreaking to emergencies to playtime so that you'll be the most prepared dog owner ever. It's all really simple once you get down in the trenches of raising your pup, but it takes work and effort, especially when it comes to training. Our hacks will cover everything you need to know to make your dog well-behaved and a good sport for years and years.

There's nothing that quite compares to that feeling you get when you're greeted by your dog after a long day. Whether your best friend joins you for a light jog, or you two share a tasty treat at night, the bond that comes with a pup is something everyone should experience. However, that bond does not start from day one. Like any great relationship, you and your new puppy will have to work together as you learn to understand and love each other.

This guide is the perfect first step to getting to know your furry pal. We've researched and tested every perspective under the sun on pet-training. The advice in this book covers the common threads within all pet owners, no matter what your breed or experience is. We can't guarantee that your dog will be the best trained one on the block, but we can give you the tools to try. So get ready to get dirty and have a blast!

"Happiness is a warm puppy."

— Charles M. Schulz

With Love
from Me to Tini & Jack
Dec. 2016

CONTENTS

PREFACE

It seems like all you need to do to bring home a puppy is buy some food and a collar, but there's a lot more to it than that. Your dog may not seem like the smartest of the bunch (or maybe it is), but either way you need to acknowledge that a dog is a living, breathing being with its own personality and needs. We've got answers to all your questions about being a dog owner. How much do I feed my dog? How do I take it on trips? How do I make my puppy internet famous?

To all these questions and more, we've got answers. Never again fear a vet visit or a flea. We've consulted the best resources out there to give you practical, easy advice to follow at every step of your dog-loving journey. We can't promise the perfect dog, but we can promise you a friend for life.

DOG
Basics

CHAPTER 1 //
Pet Basics

Pet Basics //
Why a Dog?

Dogs are adorable. Their wagging tails and big happy faces are sure to liven up your life and soul. The house is feeling a bit empty, and you think a furry buddy would really add something to your grey days. Dogs are proven to help you feel like the world is a better place, right? Well, yes. But like anything in life, having a pet takes a lot of work and responsibility. We know, we sound like parents right now.

Things to Know

Time and energy

 Dogs need a lot of both. If you're working all the time or have some other commitment, you may not be able to give a dog the love and playtime it needs to stay happy.

Money

 Dogs, like any pet, need vet visits, toys, food, training, and more. All of that costs money. For instance, if you're at work all day, can you afford to pay a dog walker?

Type of dog

If your dream is to have a Siberian husky, but you live in a tiny apartment in Florida, you may need to reconsider the dog, your location, or your housing. There are a lot of factors to consider when choosing a dog breed that will determine both your happiness and the dog's.

Age

 Dogs go through different issues at different stages of their lives. Puppies need housetraining and frequent supervision and senior dogs sometimes need special care and expensive medications. It's important to decide what age of dog will suit your needs best—a puppy isn't always the best choice.

Health and insurance

Can you keep up with the costs of keeping a dog healthy? It's not just one vet visit a year. Heartworm, flea, and other parasite prevention medications can be costly and need to be given monthly in order to avoid much nastier diseases that the critters spread. And it's a good idea to get insurance in case of an emergency. You never know when Rover will eat a stray Lego block or Tylenol pill.

Pet parenting

Dogs are really like kids, in that you can't just leave them alone and run off for a weekend getaway. Make sure you're okay with the reality of reduced spontaneity in your life.

Happiness

Research shows that dogs are proven to help you be happier and healthier throughout your life. As long as you're ready for the responsibility, there is a ton to gain from a new furry friend.

It may seem like all you need to do is take a quick trip to the pound and the pet store, but there's a lot more you should do before picking up your new friend. Read, talk to dog owners, and maybe try dog sitting a friend's pooch before getting your own.

Great Dane

Laika

Basset Hound

West Highland White Terrier

Collie Rough

Labrador Retriever

Pembroke Welsh Corgi

Bull Terrier

American Bulldog

Jack Russell Terrier

Border Collie

Mops

Chihuahua

American Foxhound

Doberman Pinscher

Dalmatian

**Pet Basics //
Choosing a Dog**

So you're ready to get a dog, but what kind will actually work for your lifestyle (and for the dog's well-being)? From Chihuahuas to Doberman Pinschers, there are endless choices for who can be the new member of your family. Choose the right dog, and you have a friend for life. Choose the wrong dog, and you'll most likely have a beloved, but stress-inducing furball to call your own. No pressure.

Types of Dogs

For Apartments

Contrary to popular belief, the issue here isn't always the dog's size, but its energy level. You'll also have to consider noise—your neighbors won't want to hear incessant barking.

Breeds: Bulldog, Shih Tzu, Pug, Bichon Frise, and Maltese.

For the Allergic

Dog allergies are very common, but never fear! We've got more than a few dog breeds that can have a place in your home. No dog is 100% dander-free (the stuff that causes your sneezing fits), but it's still possible to live a happy life with them.

Breeds: Bichon Frise, Poodle, Maltese, Bedlington Terrier, Chinese Crested, Coton De Tulear, Irish Water Spaniel, Kerry Blue Terrier, Portuguese Water Dog, Schnauzer, Xoloitzcuintli, Afghan Hound

For Families

If there are kids in your home, especially little ones, you'll need a gentle dog that's also patient with their antics. Some dogs are better suited to adults. These breeds are outgoing, friendly, and ready to love everyone they meet. Careful though, a good portion of these breeds are athletic and need a good-sized yard.

Breeds: Labrador Retriever, Bulldog, Golden Retriever, Beagle, Pug, Irish Setter, Brussels Griffon, Newfoundland, French Bulldog, Collie

For guarding your home

If you want a brave pooch to defend your home, here are a few breeds that are loyal, brave, and ready to take on anyone who comes close to their loved ones. Guard dogs, however, should go through thorough training to avoid unwanted aggressive behavior. They need to channel their smarts and toughness in a productive way.

Breeds: Bullmastiff, Doberman Pinscher, Giant Schnauzer, Akita, German Shepherd, Staffordshire Bull Terrier, Rottweiler, Puli, Rhodesian Ridgeback

For the intellectuals

Dogs are smart in their own ways, but some catch on to training and specific tasks faster than others. A really smart dog is a joy, but you'll have to take on the responsibility of getting the dog trained and keeping a steady supply of new toys to entertain Fido's mind. A bored dog will find entertainment where it can, and that may mean chewing on your favorite toys.

Breeds: Border Collie, Poodle, German Shepherd, Golden Retriever, Doberman Pinscher, Shetland Sheepdog, Labrador Retriever, Papillon, Bloodhound, Rottweiler

Other Factors

Purebred or a mix?

It's hard to tell how a dog will act and look if it isn't fully grown, so a purebred is reliable in the sense that you'll likely meet its parents before you take it home. But purebreds tend to inherit the health problems of their breed, which may mean more heartache and visits to the vet in the long run. With a mixed breed dog, you won't know exactly what they'll look like, but you may end up with a healthier dog that takes on the best aspects of its parents' breeds. No matter which one you pick, get to know them as much as possible before adopting or purchasing.

Caution! Absolutely avoid dogs from pet shops. Their puppies are likely to come from overcrowded puppy mills, where mother dogs are basically used as breeding machines to sell their babies. The result is unhappy, unhealthy puppies. Many cities are making pet shop puppies illegal.

Shelter or breeder?

 We here at Hacks headquarters have a strong preference for saving the lives of unwanted pups, so our vote goes to adopting from a shelter. Better yet, try to look for a humane society or a dedicated dog rescue. You may pay more than at the pound, but the end result is a dog that's seen a vet more than once, has its shots, is spayed and neutered, and is free (or mostly free) of icky fleas and ticks—or worse.

 That said: If your heart is really set on a purebred (and haven't found one at the shelter), make sure it's from an approved breeder registered with the American Kennel Club. Ask for a referral from veterinarians for an even more reliable source. And always visit the home of the breeder to see the conditions in which the puppies were raised.

What to look for

As we mentioned earlier, think about age, size, energy level, and personality. How shy, assertive, or friendly is the dog? Ask about the dog's behavioral history. Is it good with other pets? Does it like kids? And lastly, is it healthy?

You and your family may be anxious to bring a dog home, but it's best to do a lot of research and spend time with different dogs and puppies before you pick one. Yes, it's possible your new favorite may be adopted before you can snag it, but don't fret. According to PETA, an estimated 6 to 8 million pets enter animal shelters each year. You're likely to find more than one who is adorable enough to tug at your heart.

**Pet Basics //
Dog-Proofing the House**

Y̲ou've got a dog in mind and only have a few days left before it comes home. You may think the first thing you need to do is buy supplies, but you really should be thinking safety first. Let's dive into all the potentially terrible things that your new pup can do to itself and your home—and prevent them.

Safety First

 ### Kitchen and Bathroom

• Use childproof latches to keep little paws from prying open cabinets

• Place medications, cleaners, chemicals, and laundry supplies on high shelves

• Keep trash cans covered or inside a latched cabinet

• Check for and block any small spaces, nooks, or holes inside cabinets or behind washer/dryer units

• Make sure your kitten hasn't jumped into the dryer before you turn it on

• Keep foods out of reach (even if the food isn't harmful, the wrapper could be)

• Keep the toilet lid closed to prevent drowning or drinking of harmful cleaning chemicals

 ### Living Room

• Place dangling wires from lamps, VCRs, televisions, stereos, and telephones out of reach

• Put away children's toys and games

• Put away knick-knacks until your kitten has the coordination not to knock them over

• Check all those places where your vacuum cleaner doesn't fit, but your puppy or kitten does, for dangerous items, like string

• Move common house plants that may be poisonous out of reach. Don't forget hanging plants that can be jumped onto from nearby surfaces

• Make sure all heating/air vents have covers

• Put away all sewing and craft notions, especially thread

Garage

• Move all chemicals to high shelves or behind secure doors

• Clean all antifreeze from the floor and driveway, as one taste can be lethal to animals

• Bang on your car hood to ensure that your kitten (or any neighborhood cat) has not hidden in the engine for warmth

• Keep all sharp objects and tools out of reach

Bedroom

• Keep laundry and shoes behind closed doors (drawstrings and buttons can cause major problems if swallowed)

• Keep any medications, lotions, or cosmetics off accessible surfaces (like the bedside table)

• Move electrical and phone wires out of reach of chewing

• Be careful that you don't close your kitten in closets or dresser drawers

And look out for paws, noses, and tails when you shut doors behind you or scoot chairs!

17 POISONOUS PLANTS

LILIES

Members of the Lilium spp. are considered to be highly toxic to cats. While the poisonous component has not yet been identified, it is clear that with even ingestions of very small amounts of the plant, severe kidney damage could result.

MARIJUANA

Ingestion of Cannabis sativa by companion animals can result in depression of the central nervous system and incoordination, as well as vomiting, diarrhea, drooling, increased heart rate, and even seizures and coma.

SAGO PALM

All parts of Cycas Revoluta are poisonous, but the seeds or "nuts" contain the largest amount of toxin. The ingestion of just one or two seeds can result in very serious effects, which include vomiting, diarrhea, depression, seizures and liver failure.

TULIP/NARCISSUS BULBS

The bulb portions of Tulipa/Narcissus spp. contain toxins that can cause intense gastrointestinal irritation, drooling, loss of appetite, depression of the central nervous system, convulsions and cardiac abnormalities.

AZALEA/RHODODENDRON

Members of the Rhododenron spp. contain substances known as grayantoxins, which can produce vomiting, drooling, diarrhea, weakness and depression of the central nervous system in animals. Severe azalea poisoning could ultimately lead to coma and death from cardiovascular collapse.

OLEANDER

All parts of Nerium oleander are considered to be toxic, as they contain cardiac glycosides that have the potential to cause serious effects—including gastrointestinal tract irritation, abnormal heart function, hypothermia and even death.

CASTOR BEAN

The poisonous principle in Ricinus communis is ricin, a highly toxic protein that can produce severe abdominal pain, drooling, vomiting, diarrhea,excessive thirst, weakness and loss of appetite. Severe cases of poisoning can result in dehydration, muscle twitching, tremors, seizures, coma & death.

CYCLAMEN

Cylamen species contain cyclamine, but the highest concentration of this toxic component is typically located in the root portion of the plant. If consumed, Cylamen can produce significant gastrointestinal irritation, including intense vomiting. Fatalities have also been reported in some cases.

YEW

Taxus spp. contains a toxic component known as taxine, which causes central nervous system effects such as trembling, incoordination, and difficulty breathing. It can also cause significant gastrointestinal irritation and cardiac failure, which can result in death.

KALANCHOE

This plant contains components that can produce gastrointestinal irritation, as well as those that are toxic to the heart, and can seriously affect cardiac rhythm and rate.

AMARYLLIS

Common garden plants popular around Easter, Amaryllis species contain toxins that can cause vomiting, depression, diarrhea, abdominal pain, hypersalivation, anorexia and tremors.

AUTUMN CROCUS

Ingestion of Colchicum autumnale by pets can result in oral irritation, bloody vomiting, diarrhea, shock, multi-organ damage and bone marrow suppression.

CHRYSANTHEMUM

These popular blooms are part of the Compositae family, which contain pyrethrins that may produce gastrointestinal upset, including drooling, vomiting and diarrhea, if eaten. In certain cases depression and loss of coordination may also develop if enough of any part of the plant is consumed.

ENGLISH IVY

Also called branching ivy, glacier ivy, needlepoint ivy, sweetheart ivy and California ivy,Hedera helix contains triterpenoid saponins that, should pets ingest, can result in vomiting, abdominal pain, hypersalivation and diarrhea.

PEACE LILY
(AKA MAUNA LOA
PEACE LILY)

Spathiphyllum contains calcium oxalate crystals that can cause oral irritation, excessive drooling, vomiting, difficulty in swallowing and intense burning and irritation of the mouth, lips and tongue in pets who ingest.

POTHOS

Pothos (both Scindapsus and Epipremnum) belongs to the Araceae family. If chewed or ingested, this popular household plant can cause significant mechanical irritation and swelling of the oral tissues and other parts of the gastrointestinal tract.

SCHEFFLERA

Schefflera and Brassaia actinophylla contain calcium oxalate crystals that can cause oral irritation, excessive drooling, vomiting, difficulty in swallowing and intense burning and irritation of the mouth, lips and tongue in pets who ingest.

**Pet Basics //
Welcome Home!**

Congrats! You're officially a dog owner. Your adorable new family member needs a lot of gentle love and care during this transitional period, so don't start to worry if things aren't a perfect fit right away. Let's jump into the various ways that you can make your new friend feel at home. Have a sense of humor

New Dog Tricks

Be flexible

Your dog is a living being with its own preferences and ideas. Granted, you're the owner and can mold and train your pup to your own preferences, but that's not likely to happen right away. Maybe it wants to sleep in a different part of the house or doesn't like its food. That's okay! Have a sense of humor and be sympathetic that your new friend might be a little shocked to be in a new place.

Stock up

We've included a shopping list on the next page that has all the basics you'll need for your new friend. Remember to put a collar and ID tag on the dog immediately!

Rule time

Family meeting! Make sure everyone in your household knows what your dog is and isn't allowed to eat and do. For instance, if you don't want it jumping on the couch all the time, make that clear to your more lenient roommates (or kids).

Be loving and attentive

It's a good idea to set aside some time to give your new pet some TLC while they get used to their surroundings. They may exhibit some signs of anxiety for a few days or weeks, and that's okay. Be reassuring and avoid scolding the dog too often during this period.

Establish a schedule

 Decide when you're going to feed, walk, and play with your new dog.

Alone time

 Your dogs needs lots of love, but also some space to explore and grow confident. Watch from a distance and don't intrude if it seems to be enjoying what it's doing (and it doesn't involve your shoes).

With all these things in mind, it should be an easy transition for your dog to become a beloved member of the family. If you run into some problems, be patient and contact a vet if anything becomes unmanageable.

DOG SUPPLIES

FOOD & WATER BOWLS

COLLAR

FOUR TO SIX-FOOT LEASH

NAIL CLIPPERS

ID TAG WITH YOUR PHONE NUMBER

PHONE#

BRUSH  **OR COMB**

(Depends on your pet's coat length & type)

HARD PLASTIC CARRIER OR FOLDABLE METAL CRATE

CANINE TOOTHBRUSH & TOOTHPASTE

DOG BED

DOGGY SHAMPOO & CONDITIONER

 **SUPER-ABSORBENT PAPER TOWELS**

SPONGE & SCRUB BRUSH  **FIRST-AID SUPPLIES**

 **NON-TOXIC CLEANSER**

ENZYMATIC ODOR NEUTRALIZER

 VARIETY OF TREATS

ABSORBENT HOUSE-TRAINING PADS

 **VARIETY OF TOYS**
(a ball, rope, chew toy and puzzle toy are good starts)

BABY GATE(S)

PLASTIC POOP BAGGIES (biodegradable ones are best) or **POOPER SCOOPER**

Pet Basics //
First Vet Visit

Going to the vet doesn't have to be your pet's worst nightmare. It's a matter of finding a good vet and training your pup to be comfortable in this environment. And your pet's comfort is only one part of the equation, there are a lot of factors that go into maintaining your pet's health.

Before You Go

Find a good veterinarian

Ask your dog owner friends who they use as a vet, check reviews online, and even stop by a clinic if possible. Many practices have multiple vets, so try to go somewhere where you can request the same one each time.

Phone calls

Make sure to find a vet who doesn't mind a call once in a while, both emergency-related and for non-emergencies. Your questions are vital to making sure your pet isn't acting out of the ordinary.

Financial concerns

Consider getting health insurance. Emergencies are unpredictable, but it's likely at least one flare up will occur in your pet's lifetime. Plan ahead and set aside a thousand or more for emergencies.

Vaccinations

Vaccines are absolutely necessary for a pup's growth and health maintenance, so don't skimp on them. There are core and non-core vaccines. Core vaccines include distemper, adenovirus-2, canine parvovirus-2, and of course, rabies. Non-core vaccines are recommended based on geographic location and include leptospirosis, Lyme disease, and Bordetella. If you're getting a puppy, several rounds of booster shots will be needed, so don't skimp.

Deworming

Many puppies and dogs contract intestinal parasites from their mothers, fleas, or other dogs. It's important to have your vet conduct fecal exams and several rounds of treatment until the little buggers are gone. Roundworms, tapeworms, whipworms, and hookworms are a few of the nasty things that can hurt your pup if you don't get them in line.

Heartworm

Spread by various mosquitos, heartworm can easily kill your beloved pet. Make sure to get them on monthly medication (usually in the form of a large pill) to prevent disease. Puppies 8 weeks and older can begin the treatment.

Ectoparasites

Fleas and ticks are another major cause of health problems, so prevention is key. Ask your vet for the best topical flea and tick treatments, and make sure to wash bedding regularly and keep your grass short. Avoid taking your dog to areas where fleas and ticks thrive, like woods.

Diet and weight

Always check weight and diet recommendations with your vet. It's important to keep track of it, as many health issues that occur in overweight humans also apply to dogs as well.

Spaying and neutering

If your dog is old enough and hasn't been fixed yet, set up an appointment with your veterinarian for the surgery. It's a simple procedure and most pets heal very quickly from it.

Off to the Vet

Play vet!

The best way to get your dog or puppy accustomed to the vet experience is by handling them the way a vet would. Poke, prod, and pinch as if you were the doctor, but provide lots of treats in the process.

Drive around

One of the scary parts of the vet process may be driving in the car. Make sure to take your little fluffball on a few drives with fun destinations (like the park) before making the drive to the vet.

Bring treats to the vet

There's no better distraction.

Judge the vet

Make sure your vet is being gentle and attentive with your dog. Sometimes it isn't the dog who's being unreasonable about not wanting to be there.

Vet visits are a vital part of your dog's health, so make sure to prep beforehand to make it an easy experience for everyone. And, hopefully, you'll only have to make the trip once a year.

REASONS TO SPAY
OR NEUTER YOUR PET

1 **Your pet will be healthier.** Medical evidence proves it! In females, spaying helps prevent uterine, ovarian, and breast cancer which is fatal in about **50%** of dogs and **90%** of cats. Females spayed before their first heat **(4-5 months old)** are the healthiest, but it helps at any age. For males, especially if done before **6 months** of age, it prevents testicular cancer & prostate problems.

2 **Your pet will live longer.** Because they are healthier (see #1), spayed and neutered pets have a significantly longer average lifespan. Also, neutered pets are also less likely to roam or fight (see #4), lengthening their lifespan.

3 **Your spayed female won't go into heat.** This means you don't have to deal with blood staining, yowling, and the more frequent urination – which can be all over your house! Female felines usually go into heat four to five days every three weeks during breeding season. That's a lot of mess & noise!

4 **Your male pet is less likely to roam.** An un-neutered male pet is driven by strong hormones to mate, and will often turn into a Houdini escape artist to get out of their home or yard, especially if there is a female in heat close by, or sometimes even miles away!

5 **Your male pet will be friendlier.** A fixed male is less likely to want to fight with other pets, even females, who may not appreciate his annoying ongoing advances.

6 **Your female pet will be friendlier.** When a female pet goes into heat, the hormones can make her behavior become erratic. A usually friendly pet who goes into heat can suddenly become aggressive with both people and other pets in the home.

7 **Marking & humping will be reduced or eliminated.** This true is for both dogs and cats, and especially for males. Also male dogs will be much less likely to 'hump' other dogs… or people's legs or your couch cushions!

8 **It will save you money.** Fixed pets have fewer health problems so vet bills are lower. They are less likely to bite, avoiding potential costly lawsuits **(80% of dog bites to humans are from intact male dogs)**. They are less likely to try to escape and do damage to your home or yard, or cause a car accident.

9 **You are saving pets' lives.** You may say your pet will never get out or run away, but that's what almost every pet owner thinks – accidents happen! Pet overpopulation is a problem everywhere. **For every human born, 15 dogs & 45 cats are born.** There simply aren't enough homes for all these animals.

**CHAPTER 2 //
TRAINING**

**Training //
Housebreaking and Discipline**

Your new pup doesn't come built in with manners, so it's up to you to impart those good behaviors to your pet. It's best to go with a strategy of positive reinforcement. The standard "put his nose in it" doesn't really work. Let's go over the various problems you make run into, and find a hack for each one.

Common Bad Behavior

Poo in the wrong place

Most dogs don't want to poop where they eat, so crate training is very effective for puppies or untrained dogs. Get a crate and put your dog in it after it eats. Wait about half an hour, and then take it outside. It should have to use the bathroom. Be patient.

Tip! Make sure to never use the crate as punishment. Better yet, try to feed your dog in its crate.

Crate training

Training your dog to like his crate can have multiple uses. It becomes a quiet place to sleep or a safe place to be in if you need to go run an errand for an hour. You can't use it for everything, but it's handy, especially while the dog is learning not to chew on furniture or other bad habits. Try to place the crate somewhere where the dog can see you so it doesn't get lonely.

Tip! Try to gradually increase the intervals of time that the dog is in its crate. Your dog may whine to be let out, but ignore it until the whining stops, then let it out.

Chewing everything

If your dog is chewing all your furniture to bits, or just wants to, use crate training or simple give it its own room or closed in space. Litter the room with toys so it learns to chew on toys rather than on furniture. A destructive dog is usually a bored dog, so keep the toys and treats coming.

Hand chewing

Puppies and dogs sometimes want to play with your hands, but always direct them to a toy or treats instead. Get them used to the idea of being pet without having to mouth your hand.

Excessive barking

Dogs bark for different reasons: anxiety, playfulness, to demand attention, and boredom. Make sure your dog is getting enough exercise and avoid leaving it alone for long periods of time. **To address the problem:**

1. Never comfort your dog when it is barking for attention or out of anxiety. You're telling it that it's okay to act that way.

2. Don't shout, your dog perceives this as basically barking and sees it as encouraging.

3. Avoid punishments like shock collars. Dogs learn to get around them and they're not a kind solution.

4. Get its attention with a clap or whistle. Once it's quiet, redirect its attention to something else—like a toy or treat.

5. After getting your dog's attention, practice basic commands, like sit and down in order to shift its focus.

6. **DO NOT** let your dog bark constantly outside, regardless of the reason. Your neighbors will grow to hate your pup and maybe even call over the police.

7. Train your dog to "speak" and "be quiet." We'll look at these later in the chapter.

8. Consult your veterinarian and/or trainer if you continue to face barking issues.

Digging

Try to determine the cause of digging and work with your dog's inclinations. Does it need more exercise? More toys? Is it anxious? Is more training needed? If none of these work, train your dog to know that only a certain spot is okay for digging, like a sand box.

Separation anxiety

Is your dog tearing up the house because you're away? Crate training is one good solution for this, but there are a few other things you can do.

1. Don't make a big fuss when leaving or coming home—the dog will learn that this is a big deal and feel anxious.

2. Another tip is to do things like grabbing your keys or coat as if you were leaving, but then watch some television. That way, your dog will ease up when these things occur.

3. Lastly, for severe cases of anxiety, dedicate about an hour a day to training your dog to watch you leave. Step out of the door for a few seconds, then come back inside. Wait until your dog calms down. In a few weeks, this trick should greatly improve its separation anxiety.

Begging

Don't let it happen. Keep the dog in another room while you eat or tell it to stay in a part of the house where it can't watch you eat. If your pup behaves, give it a treat.

Chasing

Keep your dog on a leash at all times and keep a whistle on you to get its attention. It's hard to fight instinct, but eventually your dog will learn that it's not going anywhere. Try to distract it when it's trying to get away.

Jumping up

Puppies jump up to greet their moms, and later do that to people as well. Avoid lifting a knee or pushing the dog away. Jumping up is attention-seeking behavior, so the best way to fight it is by ignoring your dog. When it relaxes, give it a treat.

There's a lot for your dog to learn, but all of these behaviors are normal and can be easily corrected. Stay patient, it takes weeks, months, or even years for your dog to really become the best version of itself. And, as always, if you need help talk to a veterinarian or a trainer.

INSTINCT I.D.

Dogs are known for doing some pretty unusual things.
Have you ever wondered why? **THE ANSWER IS INSTINCT**

WHAT DOES IT MEAN WHEN MY DOG...

DIGS A HOLE?

Dogs dig for a variety of reasons many of these are instinctual. Dogs might dig as a way to cool down, bury bones or to chase prey that burrow in the ground. In fact, certain breeds were bred for digging for just this reason.

ROLLS IN SOME-THING SMELLY?

What smells terrible to you is actually quite intresting to your dog. His instincts tell him he need to share the news. By rolling in those scents, he can bring the messege back to his pack, telling them what he has found.

CIRCLES BEFORE LYING DOWN?

It's believed that this instictual behavior mimics that of dogs in the wild, who would circle in the long grass or brush to trample the area and make a soft bed.

WANTS TO LICK MY FACE?

Dogs may lick you for many reasons, includuing when they are hungry. Experts believe this behavior can be traced to the dog's days as an infant. When hungry, some pups lick their mother's nose and snout as a way of "asking" for regurgitated food. Pack members also lick each other's faces as a greeting, a way to gather information, or as a sign of submission. So your dog may want to lick your face out of instinct or he may simply be trying to get your attention.

COVERS HIS POOP?

When your dog scratches the ground after going, it's actually less of a cover-up, and more of a calling card. Dogs have scent glands in thier paws that are activated when they scratch the ground. Those marks in the grass act as an instinctual signature or signal for other dogs to find and interpret.

FIND OUT HOW TO FEED YOUR ADULT DOG'S INSTINCT.

VISIT PurinaONE.com/Instinct

Training //
Playtime

Playing with your dog seems like a no-brainer, but there are a lot of ways you can make the most out of that time—for yourself and the dog. But don't just play fetch—some dogs don't even know how to play. There are plenty of other games that you and your pup can enjoy together.

Game time!

Blanket hurdles

Clear some space in your house or yard, and place some rolled up blankets or towels to use as hurdles for your dog. Walk your dog through the course and then call it from one end to the other. Make sure to have treats at the end!

Hide and seek

Find one of your dog's favorite toys or grab a handful of treats. Have your dog sit and stay in one room and go and hide in another room. Once you've situated yourself in a good hiding place, call your dog. When it finds you, give it some treats and praise.

Treat hunt

Grab some smelly treats and hide them in a room or in the backyard. Make sure your dog is in another room while you hide them, and then bring it back in the room.

Tug of war

It may seem like a basic game, but it's a good way to channel canine aggression. Teach your dog not to grab the toy until you say "get it." Then, teach it to "let go." Reward with a treat. Once all the commands are learned, you can play tug of war.

Tip! Don't play tug of war without teaching these commands. Your dog won't learn the manners it needs to avoid being overly aggressive.

Name game

 Use two of your dog's favorite toys to start this game. Call out the name of both toys, like "duck" or "bear." Once you think your dog knows the names, put both on the ground and ask it to fetch one of them. Reward your pup when it gets it right. Once it knows those two toys, add more to its vocabulary.

Round Robin

With family or friends, sit in a large circle—maybe 15 feet apart—with a handful of treats. Everyone take a turn calling the dog's name, then reward with a treat when it goes to the right person. Your dog will love the attention, and the treats!

Frisbee toss

Pretty straightforward, but it takes a little more dexterity than "fetch." Start by playing fetch with the Frisbee, or simply rolling it toward your dog. After a while, try to toss it high in the air, so your dog will catch it.

Doggie basketball

 Grab an empty laundry basket and your dog's favorite ball. Demonstrate what you would like your dog to do. Drop the ball into the basket while saying "drop." Make sure your dog is paying attention to this command and the motion. Once you think you've done it enough times, pass the ball to your puppy player. Every time he drops the ball into the basket when you say "drop," reward him enthusiastically. It may take a while, but your pup may catch on.

There are plenty of other games you can play with your dog, so hit the Internet for some more. It's important to entertain your dog's mind, don't just toss some treats at it and call it a day. And check out our section on tricks and training—a reliable source of entertainment for your dog.

**Training //
Socialization**

Whether your dog is a full-grown or a tiny puppy, it's important to get your furball out into the world and interacting with other people and dogs. An inexperienced dog is a fearful one, and dogs that are afraid can act out in unpredictable and aggressive ways. Here are some ways to avoid that issue.

Puppy Socialization

Variety!

Make sure your puppy meets different kinds of people of different ethnicities, genders, and ages.

Pass the puppy

A good game to play with your puppy when it meets someone new is to have the person hold the puppy and give it a treat when it pets it. Have the person look in its ears, mouth, touch its tail, pet its paws, and generally get it used to be handled.

Introduce other animals

Whether it's cats, dogs, birds, or bunnies, get your puppy used to meeting all kinds of critters. Have treats nearby and teach your puppy to be respectful and not treat other smaller creatures like prey. And make sure all animals it's meeting are healthy.

Bang!

Get your puppy accustomed to different kinds of sounds. Police sirens, thunder, fire trucks, music, banging pots and pans, doorbells—all of these are noises that could potentially make your dog nervous and afraid. Get rid of those phobias with early exposure.

Nervousness

If your puppy is shy, let it explore at its own pace. Don't lure it with food, simply let it explore and praise it when it approaches the thing that's making it nervous.

Adult Socialization

Take it easy

Adult socialization is a little bit different than with a puppy. Whereas with a puppy your goal is to toss it into as many situations as possible, your first expectation with your adult dog is for it to simply be "okay" with everything. Many of the same principles that apply to puppies apply to adults, but they need to be approached differently.

Playing nice

Take your dog to a park and keep it on a leash. Let other dogs pass by at a safe distance, and if your dog barks, get its attention and walk away until it calms down. Train your pup to stay calm when other dogs are around.

Social life

If you're set on your dog playing nice with others, introduce one dog at a time, preferably a friend's dog, preferably an easygoing one. Go on a walk together to start.

Dog parks

Dog parks are a little overwhelming for a shy dog or one who's not completely socialized. Start by taking your dog on walks, then walking it on the outside of the dog park. Once your dog seems calm around other dogs, try going into the park. Make sure your dog has all its shots and is spayed or neutered.

Tip! If your dog is fearful or aggressive at the dog park, go back to calm walks and play dates. Build your way up to the dog park or know your dog's limits.

Your dog needs some kind of a social life for its well-being, but at the same time you'll need to get to know your dog's personality. It may not be very social, and that's okay. As long as you can get to the point where it's not overly aggressive, it's fine if you're your pup's best friend.

Training //
Tricks and Training

Training your dog will improve both of your lives, enhance your bond, and ensure your pup's safety—and it can provide a lot of fun and entertainment. Dogs are usually eager to learn, and the key to success is good communication. We'll start with a few basic tricks that will be the foundation for everything you'd like to teach your dog.

First Tricks

1. Clicker response

Step 1: Click and give the dog a treat.

Step 2: Repeat about two dozen times or until your dog associates the click with a treat.

Step 3: Your goal is to catch good behavior with the clicker, and reward it.

2. Name

Step 1: When your dog looks at you, click and treat.

Step 2: Repeat several times.

Step 3: Say its name as your dog looks at you.

Step 4: Repeat several times.

Step 5: Call your dog. If it looks at you, reward with a click and a treat.

3. Sit

Step 1: Wait until your dog sits on its own. Click and treat.

Step 2: Repeat several times.

Step 3: Say sit when your dog sits. Click and treat.

Step 4: Repeat!

4. Down

> **Step 1:** Grab the clicker and a treat.
>
> **Step 2:** When your dog lies down on its own, click and treat.
>
> **Step 3:** Repeat several times.
>
> **Step 4:** Start to use the command "Down
>
> **Step 5:** If your dog listens, click and treat. If not, go back to step 2.

5. Stay

> **Step 1:** Tell your dog to sit. Click and treat.
>
> **Step 2:** Say "stay." Wait a few seconds, then click and treat.
>
> **Step 3:** Continue this while increasing the time intervals.

6. Heel

> **Step 1:** Begin by having your dog on a leash.
>
> **Step 2:** If your dog pulls, don't go in that direction. Stay still.
>
> **Step 3:** When your dog is close to you with his shoulder by your left leg, click and treat.
>
> **Step 4:** When your dog starts walking regularly by your side, start saying "let's go" and "with me" so the dog associates those commands with staying by your side as you walk. If you prefer, use the word "heel."
>
> **Step 5:** Click and treat every ten steps until your dog has mastered the command.

These basic commands will ensure that your dog doesn't get into any dangerous situations, especially when you're going for walks. Make sure to go beyond these first six and teach your dog more playful tricks. It'll entertain your dog's brain and really enhance playtime.

CHAPTER 3 //
Maintenance and Nutrition

Maintenance and Nutrition //
Your Dog and Food

What should your dog eat? It's actually a more loaded question than simply going straight to the corner store and grabbing a few cans of the most popular brand. It's important to pay attention to quality, ingredients, and what's good for your dog's age, activity level, and ideal weight. With all that in mind, let's first look at the types of foods your dog can eat.

Types of Food

Dry food

Pros: Convenient for storage and feeding, cost-effective, helps to keep teeth stronger

Cons: Don't provide as much moisture as wet food

Wet food

Pros: Strong smell, increases appetite, soft for small mouths or weak and ill dogs

Cons: Can make a mess, spoils quickly, may be more expensive

Raw food

Pros: Supposedly shinier coats, healthier skin, higher energy levels

Cons: Threat of bacteria in raw meat, can lack in certain minerals and vitamins, potential for bones to choke the dog, not as convenient

Note: This diet consists of the following:

·Muscle meat, often still on the bone

· Bones, either whole or ground

· Organ meats such as livers and kidneys

· Raw eggs

· Vegetables like broccoli, spinach, and celery

· Apples or other fruit

· Some dairy, such as yogurt

How to Feed Your Dog

Measure

Use measuring cups to know how much food you're giving your dog. If you see that it's gaining weight or not enough weight, adjust accordingly. You can also contact the manufacturer for calorie information.

Activity level

Also remember to feed according to activity levels. A pampered lap dog needs less calories than an active dog who spends time running outdoors.

Two feedings

It's recommended that dogs eat twice a day, spaced eight to twelve hours apart. Fill in the gaps with the occasional treat.

Small pieces

Speaking of treats, try to use half a treat when training, or an even smaller piece. Your dog will get the point and won't be overfed.

Water!

Don't forget water. Always have a clean bowl filled with water available to your dog, especially when it's hot.

As always, talk to your vet about what they recommend for your particular dog. In the next section, we'll look at labels and how to make sense of them. For more info on what your dog can and can't eat, refer to our handy charts in this chapter.

Healthy Dog Snacks

APPLES
(No Seeds!)

BLUEBERRIES

STRAWBERRIES

GREEN BEANS

LETTUCE

SPINACH

CARROTS*
(Cooked or Raw)

WATERMELONS
(Seedless)

BANANAS*
(Try frozen for a tasty treat!)

+

PEANUT BUTTER

TRY THESE TOGETHER FOR A TASTY TREAT!

HEALTHY
WHEN COOKED

SQUASH

POPCORN*
(no butter or salt please!)

**SWEET
POTATOES**

CHICKEN
(or other cooked
meat sparingly)

NOT SAFE

TOMATOES

RAISINS

GRAPES

GARLIC

AVOCADO

ONIONS

MUSHROOMS

PITTED FRUITS
(Poison inside!)

NUTS
(Especially
Macadamia Nuts)

**CHOCOLATE
OR COCOA**
(products)

GUIDELINES

- nothing you wouldnt eat
- no seeds/pits

contact your local veterianian if you suspect
your dog are something s/he shouldn/t have.

**Maintenance and Nutrition //
Food Labels and Brands**

It's not enough just to feed your dog, you'll also need to make sure its food is nutritious. That means reading food labels and knowing which companies are tricking you into buying garbage. Let's get into how to pick the best food for your dog. Even if you spend a little more on food, it'll save you in the long run with less health problems for your pup.

Reading the Labels

Pretty words

Ignore words like "gourmet," "natural," and "premium" on the bag. Only pay attention to ingredients, as there is no standard for the use of these words, making them essentially meaningless.

Get that meat

Like human food, pet food must list ingredients by weight, starting with the heaviest. Keep in mind that meat is about 75% water, according to the FDA. If meat is high on the list, remember that it would probably be lower without water, making the food less nutritious.

Or better, protein

Look for meat meals instead, such as chicken meal or meat and bone meal. They're different as most of the water and fat have been removed, which concentrates the animal protein.

That extra stuff

Preservatives, artificial colors, and stabilizers in pet food must be either approved by the FDA or be generally recognized as safe, a category that includes everything from high fructose corn syrup to benzoyl peroxide, used to bleach flours and cheese.

Preservatives

Manufacturers must list the preservatives they add, but they do not always list preservatives in ingredients such as fish meal or chicken that are processed elsewhere.

Tip! Whether you avoid preservatives is up to you. They're generally considered safe, and they increase the shelf life of your food, helping your dog avoid spoiled food and diarrhea.

Basic nutrients

Many pet food makers follow model regulations set by the Association of American Feed Control Officials (AAFCO) that establish the minimum amount of nutrients needed to provide a complete and balanced diet.

Minimum protein

Look for the protein and fat levels on the food label. At least 10% of the daily diet, by weight, should be protein, and 5.5% should be fat, according to the National Research Council. Dog foods typically contain higher amounts than those, because dogs may not be able to digest all of the nutrients in a food.

Organic, shmorganic

Watch out for the word "organic." While in human food the U.S. Department of Agriculture has specific rules for its use, in pet food there are no such rules yet.

Cut the corn

"Corn syrup" and other corn-based products should be absent or toward the absolute bottom of the list of ingredients in your dog's food. They're often used to sweeter food or as filler, so avoid foods that list them as a top ingredient—only small amounts are healthy.

You are what you eat—and so is your dog. Make sure you're giving your dog food that gives it energy, a shiny coat, and a loving personality. Good food goes a long way to prevent your dog from getting diseases and other problems that require expensive vet visits.

NOT SURE IF YOUR DOG IS FIT OR FAT?

In general, dog owners should be able to feel their pet's ribs through a thin layer of fat and see a defined "waist" between the ribs and hips. "You should not be able to see all of a pet's ribs and spine." says Dr. Buisson. "And if you have to really press hard to find his ribs under fat, he's too big." Your veterinarian will be able to give you more accurate picture of your pet's weight and health based on individual factors; however, you can check the BCS scale to get an idea of where your pet falls on the weight spectrum:

Very Thin

1 Ribs are easy to see or feel. When viewed from above, there is an accentuated waist.

Underweight

2 Ribs are easy to feel. when viewed from above, there is an hourglass shape.

Ideal

3 Ribs can be felt. There is a slight waist when viewed from above.

Overweight

4 Ribs are difficult to feel. There are no waist when viewed from above.

Obese

5 Ribbs are very difficult to feel. When viewed from above, there is no waist and broad back.

FIT

PET GROOMING

**Maintenance and Nutrition //
Pamper and Groom**

Your dog's skin, nails, coat, teeth, and ears all need regular maintenance and cleaning, just like yours. Whether you do it yourself or have someone else do it, here are all the major areas you need to cover.

Brushing

Brush your dog's coat regularly to get rid of dirt and tangles while keeping her skin clean and irritant-free. Also use that time to check for fleas and flea dirt (little black specks).

Short, smooth coat

Use a rubber brush to loosen dead skin and dirt. Then use a bristle brush to remove dead hair. Then polish with a chamois cloth.

Short, dense coat

This type of coat is prone to matting, so use a slicker brush to remove tangles. Then catch dead hair with a bristle brush. And don't forget to comb the tail.

Long coat

On a daily basis, remove tangles with a slicker brush. Next, brush the coat with a bristle brush. Trim any excess hair around the feet.

Bathing

No need to bathe your dog often if it's mostly indoors and regular brushing takes care of the dirt. Bathe every 3 months or so. But if it's spending a lot of time outside, or even in the pool, a shampooed bath is necessary. Either way, don't do it more than every other week. Try to go for a shampoo that doesn't have fragrances or other ingredients that irritate the skin.

Ears

Don't use cotton swabs. Get a bag of cotton balls ready and an ear rinse from your pet store. Gently rub the cotton ball that's wet with ear rinse in the dog's ear, clearing out the gunk. Use multiple, especially for the inner ear. If there's a lot of gunk, more than usual, your dog may have an ear infection and needs to see the vet.

Nails

Buy some clippers at the pet store—don't use human ones. The guillotine type is easier to use. Then, place the dog on a table and stand to the side, behind the nails. Use one arm to hold the dog's head down, then the other to hold its paw. Lean your upper body on the dog if it tries to get up. Only clip the white part of the nail, not the reddish part (the quick). If you do, the nail will bleed—ouch! Leave about 2 mm of nail before the quick. If the nail is dark, cut several small cuts in order to avoid the quick.

Teeth

Brush your dog's teeth daily, or at least several times a week. Don't use human toothpaste; buy some at the pet store for dogs. Use a toothbrush, a plastic brush, or clean gauze. Give your dog treats afterward.

That's it! Those are all the basic ways to keep your dog clean and healthy. Focus particularly on the ears and teeth. It's very easy for dogs to get infections in their ears and gums. If you don't have time for all this maintenance, make sure you're having a groomer do it for you. Many groomers will even come to your house if you can't make it to the shop.

How To Clean
a dog's ears

STEP 1

Place cotton ball
with cleaning solution
in dog's earnormalities.

STEP 2

Massage the dog's
ear with cotton ball inside.

STEP 3

Let the dog shake out
excess debris.

Maintenance and Nutrition //
Getting Rid of Pests

There are so many types of fleas, ticks, parasites, and other icky things that are trying to get on your dog. You can keep your dog inside all the time, but that's unlikely. Even a 5-minute stroll to poo outside can lead to a few bugs jumping on your dog. Here area few ways to keep that from happening.

Pest Prevention

Spot-on treatments

Spot-on medications are applied monthly to the base of the neck of your dog. The medication spreads all over the body of the dog. The medicine is not affected by bathing, swimming, or rain and kills fleas and even ticks for several weeks. Read all labels and don't use on very young puppies.

Oral medications

Oral medications can be a good secondary option to use with spot-on treatments. These mainly work to disrupt the life cycle of fleas, but do not kill adult fleas on contact like spot-on treatments.

Flea shampoos

They don't last as long as the previous two options, but they work. Just know that you'll need to repeat the flea bath every two weeks

Flea collars

The effectiveness of collars depends on how invasive the fleas are in your dog's environment, and the collar needs to make contact with your dog's skin in order to transfer the chemicals to kill the fleas. This can cause an allergic reaction on the skin, so watch out for excessive scratching.

Flea dips

A dip is a concentrated chemical that needs to be diluted in water and applied to the animal's fur with a sponge or poured over the back. You do not rinse it off like a shampoo bath. Only use for severe infestations, since misuse can lead to toxic reactions. Ask your vet for advice first.

Cleaning the house

As soon as you see even a single flea (and really just regularly), do a thorough cleaning of the house every day until the infestation is under control. Vacuum every corner and along baseboards, and remember to throw away the bag when you're finished so fleas don't crawl back out. Wash and dry all of the dog's toys and bedding in hot water. And remember to vacuum the car. All of this will disrupt the flea life cycle and destroy eggs and larvae (gross, we know).

Household sprays and foggers

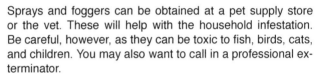

Sprays and foggers can be obtained at a pet supply store or the vet. These will help with the household infestation. Be careful, however, as they can be toxic to fish, birds, cats, and children. You may also want to call in a professional exterminator.

Clear the yard

Keep your grass short, hire an exterminator for regular yard treatments, or use yard sprays to keep pests out of the yard. Just read the labels and talk to your vet about what chemicals you're using.

Parasites

Get rid of fleas

Fleas are a leading cause of parasites like tapeworm, so make sure to take care of that issue first.

Avoid gross stuff

Train your dog to avoid eating dead animals or feces it finds on walks or in your yard, they can be infested with parasites.

Get a fecal test

Make sure to get a fecal exam at every vet visit to test for worms.

Rats and mice

 Make sure your dog isn't coming into contact with these guys, and get rid of any infestations that occur.

Symptoms

 Watch out for vomiting, diarrhea, weight loss, excessive scratching, appetite loss, or other strange behavior.

Tip! To remove a tick, get a pair of tweezers and remove at the head, the closest part to your dog's skin. Then kill the tick in rubbing alcohol. The same can be done with fleas.

You'll have bright summer days ahead of Frisbee tossing, swimming, hiking, or just strolls to the park if you follow these tips. Make sure to check your dog after every outing and stop an infestation before it starts.

Maintenance and Nutrition //
Spotting a Problem

Dogs tend to hide when they're sick, so it's often hard to tell when something is wrong until it's gotten serious. Make sure you know some of the common signs of when your pup's health may be in trouble. And don't hesitate to call your vet with questions.

Common Signs of Trouble

- Bad breath or drooling

- Excessive drinking or urination

- Appetite change associated with weight loss or gain

- Change in activity level (e.g., lack of interest in doing things they once did)

- Stiffness or difficulty in rising or climbing stairs

- Sleeping more than normal, or other behavior or attitude changes

- Coughing, sneezing, excessive panting, or labored breathing

- Dry or itchy skin, sores, lumps, or shaking of the head

- Frequent digestive upsets or change in bowel movements

- Dry, red, or cloudy eyes

 Tip! Much like WebMD, PetMD exists and also has a symptom checker for your pet. Just don't think that every symptom points to cancer.

Common Illnesses

Ear infections

- Head shaking or head tilting

- Ear odor

- Vigorous scratching

- Lack of balance

- Unusual back-and-forth eye movements

- Redness of the ear canal

    - Swelling of the outer portion of the ear

    - Brown, yellow, or bloody discharge

Worms

- Diarrhea (may be bloody)
- Weight loss
- A change in appetite
- A rough, dry coat
- Scooting on his bottom
- An overall poor appearance

Fleas

- Excessive scratching, licking, or biting at the skin
- Hair loss
- Hot spots
- Allergic dermatitis
- Tapeworms (which are carried by fleas)
- Flea dirt (looks like small black dots) against your dog's skin

Memorize these signs and you'll be ahead of the curve when your pooch is sick. The earlier you spot illness, the quicker and cheaper it is to treat in your best friend.

THE TOP 10+
SIGNS YOUR
DOG MAY BE SICK

SYMPTOMS

Regardless of your dog's age, you play a key role in helping her combat illness and remain as healthy as possible. Remember, your dog cannot describe symptoms to you, but she can show you signs of disease. Awareness of the signs of the most common diseases is one way to help reduce your pet's risk of being affected by them. It's a little scary to consider that 10% of pets that appear healthy to their owners and their veterinarians during annual checkups have underlying diseases.

SIGNS

🐾 Bad breath or drooling.

🐾 Excessive drinking or urination.

🐾 Appetite change associated with weight loss or gain.

🐾 Change in activity level.
(e.g., lack of interest in doing things they once did).

🐾 Stiffness or difficulty in rising or climbing stairs.

🐾 Sleeping more than normal, or other behavior or attitude changes.

🐾 Coughing, sneezing, excessive panting, or labored breathing.

🐾 Dry or itchy skin, sores, lumps, or shaking of the head.

🐾 Frequent digestive upstest or change in bowel movements.

🐾 Dry, red, or cloudy eyes.

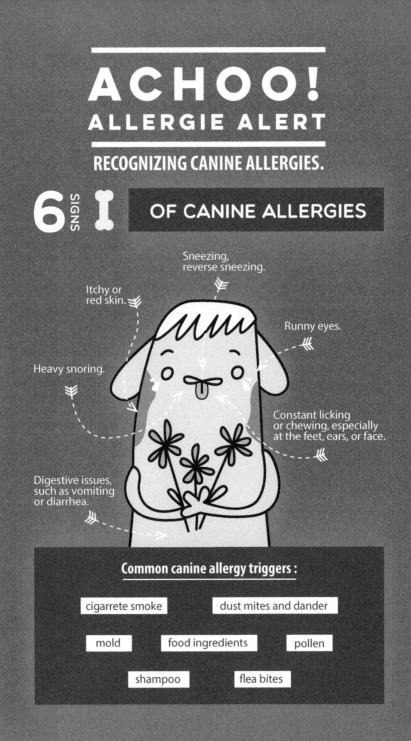

Conquering canine allergies

DISCUSS
your pets symptoms with your vet.

USE
veterinarian-recommended flea and tick control products regularly.

CLEAN
your dog's bedding weekly.

BATHE
your dog regularly with hypoallergenic shampoo.

ASK
your veterinanrian about anthistamines, ear cleaners, and antisepticskin wipes.

WORK
with your vet to keep your pet's skin clean, dry, and free of bacterial and yeast infection.

IF
food allergy is suspected work with your vet tostablish a hydrolyzed protein diet.

CONSIDER
allergy testing and hyposensitization treatment if the steps above stop working well.

CHAPTER 4 //
Pet Problems

**Pet Problems //
First Aid**

Home care should never be a replacement for veterinary care, but you can do a lot to help your dog before you get it to the emergency room. Here are a few common situations you may run into along the road of dog ownership.

Common Emergencies

Poisoning

If you pet's skin or eyes are exposed to a toxic product, check the label for the instructions for exposure. If it says to wash hands with soap and water, do the same to your pet. Don't get any soap into its eyes, nose, or mouth. If the instructions call for it, flush your pet's eyes out with water, then call the vet immediately.

If your pet is having a seizure or losing consciousness, call the vet immediately, or the Animal Poison Control Center at 888.426.4435.

Have the following information available:

Species, breed, age, sex, weight and number of animals involved.

Symptoms

Name/description of the substance that is in question; the amount the animal was exposed to; and the length of time of the exposure (how long it's been since your pet ate it or was exposed to it).

- Have the product container/packaging available for reference.
- Collect any material your dog may have eaten in a plastic bag for your vet to examine.

Seizures

- Keep your pet away from any objects (including furniture) that might hurt it. Do not try to restrain the pet.
- Time the seizure (they usually last 2-3 minutes).
- After the seizure has stopped, keep your pet as warm and quiet and contact your veterinarian.

Fractures

- Muzzle your pet.
- Gently lay your pet on a flat surface for support.
- While getting your injured pet to a veterinarian, use a board or other firm surface as a stretcher, or use a throw rug or blanket as a sling. Secure the pet with a blanket.
- Leave the bandaging and splinting to a veterinarian.

Bleeding (external)

- Muzzle your pet.
- Press a clean, thick gauze pad over the wound, and keep pressure over the wound with your hand until the blood starts clotting. This will often take several minutes. Hold pressure on it for a minimum of 3 minutes and then check it.
- If bleeding is severe and on the legs, apply a tourniquet (using an elastic band or gauze) between the wound and the body, and apply a bandage and pressure over the wound.
- Loosen the tourniquet for 20 seconds every 15-20 minutes. Severe bleeding can quickly be life-threatening—get your animal to a veterinarian immediately if this occurs.

Bleeding (internal)

Symptoms

Bleeding from nose, mouth, rectum, coughing up blood, blood in urine, pale gums, collapse, weak and rapid pulse.

- Keep animal as warm and quiet as possible and transport immediately to a veterinarian.

Chemical

- Muzzle the animal.
- Flush burn immediately with large quantities of water.

Severe

- Muzzle the animal.
- Quickly apply ice water compress to burned area.

Symptoms

Difficulty breathing, excessive pawing at the mouth, choking sounds when breathing or coughing, blue-tinged lips/tongue.

- Use caution – a choking pet is more likely to bite in its panic.
- If the pet can still breathe, keep it calm and get it to a veterinarian.
- Look into the pet's mouth to see if a foreign object is visible. If you see an object, gently try to remove it with pliers or tweezers, but be careful not to push the object further down the throat. Don't spend a lot of time trying to remove it if it's not easy to reach.
- If you can't remove the object or your pet collapses, place both hands on the side of your pet's rib cage and apply firm quick pressure, or lay your pet on its side and strike the rib cage firmly with the palm of your hand 3-4 times. The idea behind this is to sharply push air out of their lungs and push the object out from behind. Keep repeating this until the object is dislodged or until you arrive at the veterinarian's office.

For other emergencies, get on the phone with your vet or an emergency animal clinic immediately. Don't try to solve a problem yourself or use Google. Always consult a professional first, and try to keep your dog from injuring itself further. And remember, stay calm.

Pet Problems //
Finding a Lost Pet

Iit's terrible, but it happens. Sometimes your pet will dig a hole in your yard or run off in the middle of the night. Maybe someone left a door open for too long. Whatever the reason, you can't find your dog and it's a terrible feeling. Let's look at the different ways to get your pup back.

Lost and Found

Microchip

 If your dog has a microchip, and it should, make sure to go on the chip manufacturer's website and update your dog's profile. If it allows you to, put out an alert that your dog is missing.

Hide and seek

 Ask your family or roommates when they last saw the dog. Search your home carefully. Take a slow walk or ride around the neighborhood. Ask friends or neighbors if they've seen your dog, and bring a recent photo. Ask them to check their homes as well.

Pick up the phone

Call shelters, human societies, animal control agencies, rescue groups, and even the police to inquire about your dog. If possible, go in person with a picture of your pet. Some shelters have websites where you can check for recently found pets.

Flyers

It's traditional, but it works. Create both a print and digital "lost dog" flyer to get your pet back. Spread them around the neighborhood. Use social media to call attention to friends and family. Some local shelters and rescue groups have social media pages as well, make sure to give them a heads up as well.

Offer a reward

People may take more notice if you offer a reward, but it's up to you whether to do so.

It's tough to lose a pet, but don't give up! Many dogs have found their way home after long periods of time.

TIPS FOR RECOVERING
A LOST PET

Loosing your pet could be a terrifying and traumatic ordeal. Here are some expert tips proven to help you and your pet reunite.

MAINTAIN
a base where your pet dissapeard. Be sure to leave something with your scent there.

make large posters that say
REWARD

CREATE
Fliers or business cards. Hand them out in frequented areas

Your pet should have a
MICROCHIP
in addition to a
PET ID TAG

CALL • BEFRIEND VISIT • • • • • • • •
Area veterianrians & shelters.

STAY CONNECTED
post on facebook, twitter, craiglist & any other internet sites that may be helpful.

Pet Problems //
Caring for an Aging Dog

The years will pass and your young puppy will eventually become an old, wizened hound. Of course, you won't love your pet any less, but the way you care for and maintain your pet may change. Older pets require different food, more vet visits, and more TLC. Here are some things to expect as your dog ages.

DOG YEARS	HUMAN YEARS (*dog size lbs)
07	Small – Medium: 44-47 Large – Very large: 50-56
10	Small – Medium: 56-60 Large – Very large: 66-78
15	Small – Medium: 76-83 Large – Very large: 93-115
20	Small – Medium: 96-105 Large: 120

Senior Pet Care

Common health problems

Older dogs get a lot of the problems that old humans get, like cancer, heart disease, kidney and urinary tract disease, liver disease, diabetes, joint or bone disease, senility, and weakness.

Increased veterinary care

Vet visits should become semi-annual instead of annual so that illnesses can be detected sooner.

Diet and nutrition

Make sure to buy "senior" food for your pet. These will be easier to digest, have different calorie levels, and anti-aging nutrients.

Weight control

An overweight dog is more likely to have joint problems or even diabetes, both extremely detrimental to its health. Make sure to feed the correct food and portions according to your vet's recommendations.

Parasite control

 Older pets' immune systems are not as strong as younger pets, so keep an eye out for parasite symptoms.

Mobility

 Light and regular exercise will keep your pet healthier and less likely to have joint problems, like arthritis.

Vaccinations

 Talk to your vet about your older pet's changing vaccine needs.

Mental health

 Pets can show signs of senility. Stimulate them with toys, training, and treats to keep them mentally active.

Environment

Older pets may need to spend more time indoors and may need things like a memory foam mattress bed to rest sore joints.

Reproductive diseases

Pets that haven't been spayed or neutered are at greater risk of mammary, testicular, and prostate cancers.

Behavioral Changes

- Increased reaction to sounds
- Increased vocalization
- Confusion
- Disorientation
- Decreased interaction w/humans
- Increased irritability
- Decreased response to commands
- Increased aggressive/protective behavior
- Increased anxiety
- House soiling

- Decreased self-hygiene/grooming
- Repetitive activity
- Increased wandering
- Change in sleep cycles

As always, your vet is the best resource for what changes are happening to your pet as it gets older. This is also a great time to invest in insurance (or maybe a few years earlier) as maintaining your dog's health will take a greater toll on your wallet than in previous years. But, of course, you'll do it with love!

GIVING UP A *Dog*

Pet Problems //
Giving Up a Dog

For whatever reason—financial reasons, lifestyle changes, or specific pet behavior problems—it may be necessary to re-home your dog. It's an unpleasant decision for everyone, but if it's in the best interest of your pet, it's worth doing. Here are some reasons that people consider re-homing, and the best ways to go about it.

Why Re-Home?

Behavior problems

 Whether it's a new baby on the way, destructive chewing, or aggressiveness toward another pet, there are ways to solve your dog's behavior problems before you consider giving it up. Talk to an animal behaviorist or your vet. Find an animal behaviorist at www.certifiedanimalbehaviorist.com.

Renting

If a landlord is the problem, create a "resume" for your dog, complete with an adorable photo, to help with the application process.

Temporary issues

If there's a big change happening in your life, ask a friend or family member to temporarily care for the dog until things have settled.

Your search

If you really can't find a solution for your problems, prepare your dog for re-homing by doing the following:

1. Spay or neuter your pet if you haven't already
2. Update your pet's vaccinations
3. Take good photos and write detailed info about your dog
4. Spread the word on social media and flyers, as you would for a lost dog
5. Charge fee, to avoid people with bad intentions

Tip! Donate the fee to an animal shelter if you don't need it.

Choosing the right home

 Ask as many questions as possible from your new owners and schedule a home visit. Here are some sample questions:

- Why are you interested in my dog? What specifically attracts you to her?

- Where will the dog live during the day?

- Where will she sleep at night?

- What kind of activities do you want to do with the dog? Do you plan on training her? If so, how?

- Where will you take the dog for veterinary care?

- Do you have any other pets? Do you have a family or roommates living with you?

- Have you ever had a dog before? If so, what happened to him or her? You can also ask to see veterinary records for previous pets to verify that they received proper care.

- What would you do if you had to give up the dog for some reason in the future? Let the prospective adopter know if you're willing to take your dog back in the event that things don't work out.

Shelters and rescue groups

 It's best not to give up your pet to already overcrowded shelters, but some rescue groups and humane societies offer re-homing services or will aid your search while you still have your dog in your possession.

Whatever you do, don't "set your dog free." Domestic dogs can't fend for themselves. And don't re-home your pet without giving all relevant information. Lastly, stay in touch with your new dog's owners. You'll have peace of mind and maybe a cute Christmas card to look forward to each year.

Pet Problems //
Off to Sleep

The hardest thing in owning a dog is losing your best friend. We've been there, and it's never easy. While you and your vet need to make the choice of the way your pet will pass on, if you get to make that choice, we're going to go over some of the ways you can grieve in a healthy way.

Understanding Grief

Putting a pet to sleep

If you get the choice to do so, think about whether it's the best choice for your pet, particularly if it's unable to enjoy the activities it used to or is in extreme pain.

Acknowledge your pain

For many people, a dog is not "just a dog." He or she was your friend, companion, and a member of your family. Most people understand this, but if you're afraid of what your workplace will think, simply take a sick day or two. Allow yourself some down time while you cope with this difficult reality.

Pain is normal

Whether you feel something or nothing at all, everyone grieves differently. Your feelings may go haywire and be very extreme or numb, all of that is normal.

Find friends

Seek out people who loved your pet too, or who have also lost pets. They'll be the most compassionate to your pain.

Feel how you feel

Don't let anyone tell you how to feel. Your grief is your own, and anyone who doesn't understand that can buzz off.

Rituals help

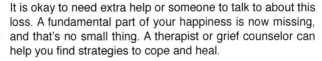

A funeral, cremation, or other type of grieving and memorial process can help you find some closure and dedicate something special to your pet.

With other pets

Try to maintain a normal routine, as your surviving pets will note your sorrow and they may also notice the missing pet. And take care of yourself as well.

Seek professional help

It is okay to need extra help or someone to talk to about this loss. A fundamental part of your happiness is now missing, and that's no small thing. A therapist or grief counselor can help you find strategies to cope and heal.

Take joy in little things

Try to find the joy that you got from your pet in other places, or in memories of your pet.

Children

If you have a child, make them a part of the grieving process and even the funeral. Reassure your child that it's okay to be sad. Don't rush out to get a replacement pet, as it may make everyone uncomfortable.

It's not easy, but it is possible to bounce back from a pet's death. They'll always have a place in your heart, even if you decide to get a new pet. Keep mementos and pictures of your old dog to remember those special moments.

CHAPTER 5 //
Modern Pet

**Modern Pet //
Traveling with Your Dog**

The modern dog isn't just a lap dog waiting at home for you to come home. Take your pup out on the town! Or to another country! There are plenty of tools and services that help you do just that. Make the most of your time with your favorite family member and let it explore too.

Prepping for Travel

Health and safety

Bring your dog to the vet for a check up and ask for copies of all its records. Make sure all vaccinations are up-to-date. Airlines will ask for health certification. Pack enough of your dog's regular food, bottled water, and any medications needed.

Crate

A crate is required for airline travel, and the best way to keep your dog safe for extended car travel. It's also handy when you're staying in hotels and don't want your pooch to make a mess.

Tip! A crate should be large enough for your dog to stand, turn, and lie down.

Tip! Make sure to include a "Live Animal" label on the crate.

Identification

Make sure your dog has its leash and collar with ID tags. A microchip is a good idea as well. Have a recent picture of your dog with you.

Hotel

Find out in advance which hotels on your route will allow dogs. Keep your dog as quiet as possible and never leave it unattended. Leave the room as clean as you found it.

Supplies

There are plenty of cute travel supplies for dogs, some of which you may want to invest in. First and foremost is a portable or collapsible food and water bowl. Doggie backpacks can be handy as well. And remember to bring lots of toys and treats for the ride.

Travel Methods

 By car

Get your dog used to the car by letting it sit with you in the driveway, then going for short rides.

Avoid carsickness by letting it travel on an empty stomach.

Do not let the dog stick its head out the window—this can lead to eye injuries.

Never leave your dog unattended in a closed vehicle or even with the windows cracked open. Within minutes, your dog can die from overheating.

 By plane

Airline rules

Each airline has its own set of rules, so call ahead to see what they require.

Tip! Before buying a crate, see what will fit the requirements of most airlines.

By train, bus, and boat

Trains

 Dogs are not allowed on Amtrak trains, unless they are service dogs.

Buses

 They also aren't allowed on Greyhound or other interstate bus companies. Local rail and bus companies may have different policies.

Cruises

 Each cruise has different policies, but some are dog-friendly.

With some proper training and preparation, traveling with your dog can be a breeze. If you want to take your dog to another country, it can be a challenge as customs laws vary widely for different countries. Take this into account when planning your dream trip. If you can't bring your bud along, leave it with a trusted friend, pet sitter, or well-recommended dog kennel.

DID YOU KNOW?

Dogs are more prone to heat stroke because they don't sweat like us. They mainly cool themselves through panting.

Heatstroke is serious and scary. It can lead to organ failure and death if not treated right away.

EARLY WARNING SIGNS YOUR DOG IS OVERHEATING

HOW TO KEEP YOUR DOG COOL

Acts sluggish or confused

Panting hard

Tongue appears bright red

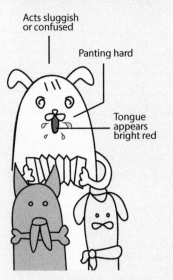

1.

Get your dog a cooling bed, pad or mat.

2.

Get your dog a good dog house or dog tent to keep the sun off them.

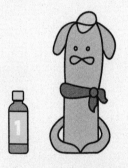

Tie a wet bandana
around your dog's neck.

Get a kiddy pool for your
dog to splash around in.

Set up a fan, so air circulates
where your dog hangs out.

Always make shure your dog
has fresh water and shade.

Modern Pet //
Sports and Outdoors

Dogs love to be outside, but since they're not as well prepared for it as their wolf ancestors are, it's up to you to fill the gaps. Make sure your cuddly furball is trained and ready to go before heading out into the great outdoors.

Into the Wild

Rules

Know the rules related to whichever campsite or RV park you're going to. If they are allowed, ask for specific rules, like what to do with their waste. Many national parks restrict dog access, but state parks can be more lenient.

Pest prevention

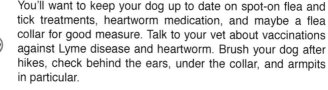

You'll want to keep your dog up to date on spot-on flea and tick treatments, heartworm medication, and maybe a flea collar for good measure. Talk to your vet about vaccinations against Lyme disease and heartworm. Brush your dog after hikes, check behind the ears, under the collar, and armpits in particular.

Tip! Don't forget about larger pests. Keep them away by putting food away at night.

Train

Basic obedience training will go a long way to keep your dog safe. "Come" should be one that comes easily to your dog by now. The other basics we talked about earlier are vital, too. And without a doubt, keep your dog on a leash at all times.

Pack a doggie bag

Make sure to bring all the basics: food, water, a first aid kit, ID tags, and bedding. There's also dog-safe sunscreen, blinking LED collar lights, booties, high visibility jackets, and life vests for water activities. And bring some toys, Frisbees in particular.

Outdoor Activities

Hiking

Before hiking, you'll need to condition your dog to take a five-mile trek. And check with your vet to see if your dog is too old or young for such heavy activity. Growing bones and old bones alike aren't made for rough terrain. Like you would with a person, start them off on lighter, more even paths.

Tip! Always clean up after your pet. No one wants to step in its poop—or smell it.

Jogging

The same advice applies as if your dog was hiking. And make sure that your dog is a running breed, some are more prone to respiratory and overheating issues, like Pugs and Bulldogs. Keep your dog on a leash and make sure the pavement isn't too hot for your dog's paws. Check your dog's paws after the run for debris that may have gotten stuck in there.

Tip! A good way to test if the sidewalk is too hot is to put your palm face down on the sidewalk. If it's too hot for your hand, it's too hot for your dog's paws.

Swimming

Some breeds of dogs can swim like fish, while others can't. Regardless, you'll want to outfit your dog with a life vest so it doesn't sink right to the bottom. After that, you can try to teach your dog to swim in a shallow area, gradually taking it to deeper water. Support your dog's belly with an arm if it needs it. Always rinse your dog with fresh water afterward to get rid of chemicals or algae clinging to the coat. And reward with praise and a treat for a job well done.

There are a lot of intensive activities to do with your dog, like agility training, but these are a good start to give your dog a well-balanced workout routine.

Modern Pet //
Becoming a Therapy Dog

If you'd like to contribute and help people with your dog, becoming a therapy dog is a great option. A therapy dog is trained to provide affection and comfort to people in hospitals, retirement homes, schools, hospices, disaster areas, and people with learning difficulties. Unlike a service dog, which require intensive training for a specific purpose, like serving the blind, any dog can be a therapy dog with the proper certification.

Getting Certified

Doggy personality

Make sure your dog is the outgoing, friendly kind. If your dog is shy or simply tolerant of new situations, it's not going to be a fun experience for either of you

Organizations

Here are a list of places where you can get your dog certified:http://www.akc.org/events/title-recognition-program/ therapy/organizations/

Training

Training may take anywhere from 10 to 15 hours or more, so prepare for a big time commitment for a few weeks.

Basic obedience

If your dog already knows basic obedience commands, like "sit," "stay," and "down," it'll be a step ahead in its training. Regardless, it'll have to learn these commands to be certified.

Environment

The dog will become familiarized with hospital equipment and undergo socialization exercises with dogs and people to get it used to novel stimuli.

Therapy training

This portion contains meeting and greeting exercises, further familiarization with the hospital environment, role-playing in this environment, and instruction and coaching on safe dog handling in health care facilities (that part is for you to learn).

Get out there

The organization you trained with will likely put you in touch with the appropriate facilities that want therapy dogs.

And that's it! Your local organization will also help you out with any needed certification with organizations like Therapy Dogs International (http://www.tdi-dog.org/), who will make your dog's status official. After that, you and your dog get to have the rewarding and fun experience of helping those in need of extra puppy love.

Modern Pet //
The Internet-Famous Dog

Don't let your dog just sit there eating your food and love all the time. Turn them into an Internet star and make some serious bank off of its inherent cuteness and hilarity.

Walk of Fame

Cute name

You may have named your dog something less than memorable, so give it a stage name. Something cute like "Boo" or "Maru."

Start young

People love puppies and kittens, and that age group tends to be the most spontaneous and silly. Record your pup doing as many adorable things as possible.

Stairs

The classic "climbing down the stairs for the first time" video will be a surefire first hit.

Weird world

What's different about your pet? Its bark? Its inability to catch a single treat in its mouth, ever? Does it talk (sort of)? Find that special something and make, like, a million videos about it.

Interests

What makes them happiest in the world? Is it their ability to jump headfirst into a box? Adorably belly flopping into water? Find out what your dog's favorite weird interest is.

Cuddles

Even cuddling with a toy will make a great video. 1 million hits!

Translate your pet's thoughts

If you're handy with video editing and Photoshop, this is another amusing viral video idea.

Or a song

A silly song about your pet's antics, set to Beyonce preferably. Or whatever the Internet loves these days.

It's improbable, but even you can make a small fortune off the cuteness of your pets. Disabled cat Lil Bub has her own documentary, a book deal, a web TV show, and stuffed animals of herself. That could be you and ol' Rover someday, you never know.

**Modern Pet //
Pet Tech**

H ey, it's the 21st century, and your dog doesn't care about your iPad. You'll need to get it its own set of cool toys to play with. And, of course, there's an app for everything related to keeping your pooch healthy and happy. Let's take a look at some of the best.

Techno-Dog

iFetch

The iFetch will set you back $100, but it shoots a ball 10 to 30 feet away, taking the strain out of your throwing arm.

Passport Pet Access Smart System Door

This is straight out of Star Trek, costs $230 dollars, an is a special door that allows pets only to pass through the door if their collar has a special passport key attached. You can even change the settings remotely.

Petnet SmartFeeder

It costs $249 and it's basically a fancy, cool-looking bowl. The times and portions that your dog gets fed are programmed through a computer, smartphone, or tablet, and calorie in-take can be monitored on a daily, weekly, or monthly basis.

Whistle Activity Monitor

This $130 collar attachment monitors your dogs weight, age, and breed to calculate periods of activity and rest. You can also set and chart health goals and track behavior patterns.

PetChatz

A $349 dollar Facetime device, this video device allows you and your pet to see each other, dispense treats remotely, and records videos of your pet.

Owner Apps

To Do

A simple "to do" app will remind you of when to feed, walk, and play with your dog. A regular schedule is important, especially for training and behavior modification.

Spending

A good budget app like Spending on My Dog will help you keep track of the expenses on your dog, and see where you may need to make some adjustments.

Dog park

Dog park finder apps help you find great places for your pup to hang out. Dog Park by Dogster.com even has social tools for chatting up and meeting other puppy parents.

Health and emergencies

PetMD's Dog First Aid can lead you through many of the emergencies we talked about earlier, and then some.

Services

How do you find a doggy daycare or a groomer? Pet MD's Pet Services Finder will help you out there. All of your pet needs are at a touch of your finger.

There are tons of other tools out there, so find the ones that work for you. And don't think you need to spend on expensive dog gadgets, they're just fun things you may want to splurge on one Christmas.

Owning a dog is wonderful and sometimes overwhelming, but it's also one of the most rewarding relationships you'll ever have. These hacks are intended to keep you and your dog open to new adventures, but also safe. Don't go with your gut when it comes to dog care. You can never be too careful when it comes to your best friend, so always contact a vet when something seems off. While we've done our best to be as thorough as possible in describing all the ups-and-downs you may encounter, the truth is that life is unpredictable. We hope you give our hacks a shot, tweet the ones you love (#DogHacks) and write to us @ mangomediainc about your weird, sweet, and silly dog owner stories. Good luck with your new best friend!

DATA SOURCES

https://www.aspca.org/pet-care/animal-poison-control/17-poisonous-plants

http://media.mnn.com/assets/images/2015/04/tumblr_inline_muttTmagp01qzo0n7.jpg

http://www.cincinnatilabrescue.org/wp-content/uploads/dog-healthy-food.jpg

https://www.pinterest.com/pin/449023025317784262/

https://advancedtutresofadogmom.files.wordpress.com/2013/08/infographic_instinct_lid.jpg

https://www.pinterest.com/pin/335090250285003689927/

https://www.pinterest.com/pin/464996730253827399/

https://www.pinterest.com/pin/26831609027538477399/

https://www.pinterest.com/pin/511580838893461818/

https://www.pinterest.com/pin/757872062011812711/

OTHER SOURCES

http://www.petmd.com/dog/care/evr_dg_before-getting_a_dog

http://www.akc.org/dog-owners/responsible-dog-ownership/#getready

http://www.humanesociety.org/animals/dogs/tips/choosing_dog.html?referrer=https://www.google.com

http://www.akc.org/dog-breeds/

http://www.humanesociety.org/animals/dogs/tips/choosing_dog.html?referrer=https://www.google.com/

http://www.americanhumane.org/animals/adoption-pet-care/safety/pet-proofing-your-home.html?referrer=https://www.google.com/

http://www.adoptapet.com/blog/10-tips-for-welcoming-home-your-newly-adopted-dog/

http://pets.webmd.com/dogs/features/making-the-most-of-your-vet-visit

https://www.petfinder.com/pet-adoption/dog-adoption/pet-adoption-checklist/

http://www.cesarsway.com/dog-care/puppies/top-10-checklist-for-your-puppy

http://www.quickanddirtytips.com/pets/dog-behavior/keep-your-dog-calm-when-visiting-the-vet

https://www.aspca.org/pet-care/virtual-pet-behaviorist/dog-behavior/house-training-your-adult-dog

http://dogs.about.com/od/dogtraining/tp/behaviorproblems.htm

http://mom.me/pets/dogs/17986-beyond-fetch-10-other-games-play-your-dog/item/name-game/

http://www.nylabone.com/dog-101/training-behaviors/socializing-your-puppy/

http://www.quickanddirtytips.com/pets/dog-behavior/how-to-socialize-your-puppy

http://www.animalhumanesociety.org/training/socializing-adult-dog

http://www.cesarsway.com/dog-training/socialization/how-to-socialize-an-adult-dog

https://www.doggiebuddy.com/topics/Trainingtopics/Traintopic3.html

http://pets.webmd.com/dogs/guide/best-dog-food-choices

https://www.aspca.org/pet-care/dog-care/feeding-your-adult-dog

http://pets.webmd.com/dogs/guide/how-to-read-a-dog-food-label

https://www.aspca.org/pet-care/dog-care/grow-your-dog

https://www.aspca.org/pet-care/virtual-pet-behaviorist/dog-behavior/brushing-your-dogs-teeth

http://www.petmd.com/dog/parasites/evr_dg_10_ways_to_stop_fleas_from_biting_your_dog

http://pets.webmd.com/dogs/6-most-common-dog-health-problems

https://www.avma.org/public/EmergencyCare/Pages/Basic-Pet-First-Aid-Procedures.aspx

https://www.aspca.org/pet-care/finding-lost-pet

httpo://www.avma.org/public/PetCare/Pages/Caring-for-an-Older-Pet-FAQs.aspx

https://www.aspca.org/pet-care/virtual-pet-behaviorist/dog-behavior/re-homing-your-dog

http://www.akc.org/dog-owners/responsible-dog-ownership/travel-tips/

http://www.cesarsway.com/dog-training/walking/the-great-outdoors

http://www.sparkpeople.com/blog/blog.asp?post=10_tips_for_running_with_your_dog

http://www.businessinsider.com/how-to-turn-your-pet-into-a-youtube-star-2013-1?op=1

http://www.housebeautiful.com/shopping/home-gadgets/tips/g1683/pet-technology/

http://www.petmd.com/dog/puppycenter/top_tens/evr_dg_best_puppy_apps_smart_phone